EASY INSTRUMENTAL DUETS

TROMBONES

BROADWAY SONGS FOR TWO

Arrangements by Peter Deneff

ISBN 978-1-5400-1287-6

HAL•LEONARD®

7777 W. Bluemound Rd. P.O. Box 13819 Milwaukee, WI 53213

CONTENTS

ANY DREAM WILL DO

from JOSEPH AND THE AMAZING TECHNICOLOR® DREAMCOAT

TROMBONES

Music by ANDREW LLOYD WEBBER
Lyrics by TIM RICE

20
24
28
32
36
40

BRING HIM HOME

from LES MISÉRABLES

TROMBONES

Music by CLAUDE-MICHEL SCHÖNBERG
Lyrics by HERBERT KRETZMER
and ALAIN BOUBLIL

21
25
29
D.S. al Coda
CODA
37
rit.
rit.

CABARET

from the Musical CABARET

TROMBONES

Words by FRED EBB
Music by JOHN KANDER

20
24
28
32
36
40

EDELWEISS

from THE SOUND OF MUSIC

TROMBONES

Lyrics by OSCAR HAMMERSTEIN II
Music by RICHARD RODGERS

26
31
35
39
44
rit.
rit.

FOR FOREVER
from DEAR EVAN HANSEN

TROMBONES

Music and Lyrics by BENJ PASEK
and JUSTIN PAUL

16
19
22
25
28
31

HELLO, DOLLY!

from HELLO, DOLLY!

TROMBONES

Music and Lyric by
JERRY HERMAN

21
25
29
1.
33
2.
37

I BELIEVE

from the Broadway Musical THE BOOK OF MORMON

TROMBONES

Words and Music by TREY PARKER, ROBERT LOPEZ and MATT STONE

Moderately

26
31
36
41
46
51

I WHISTLE A HAPPY TUNE

from THE KING AND I

TROMBONES

Lyrics by OSCAR HAMMERSTEIN II
Music by RICHARD RODGERS

22
26
31
36
41
45

IF I WERE A BELL

from GUYS AND DOLLS

TROMBONES

By FRANK LOESSER

17
21
25
29
33
rit.
rit.

THE IMPOSSIBLE DREAM
(The Quest)
from MAN OF LA MANCHA

TROMBONES

Lyric by JOE DARION
Music by MITCH LEIGH

18
21
24
27
30
33
rit.
rit.

MAMMA MIA

from MAMMA MIA!

TROMBONES

Words and Music by BENNY ANDERSSON,
BJÖRN ULVAEUS and STIG ANDERSON

21
24
27
31
35
39

MEMORY

from CATS

TROMBONES

Music by ANDREW LLOYD WEBBER
Text by TREVOR NUNN after T.S. ELIOT

Slowly, with feeling

22
26
30
35
39
43

MY FAVORITE THINGS

from THE SOUND OF MUSIC

TROMBONES

Lyrics by OSCAR HAMMERSTEIN II
Music by RICHARD RODGERS

25
32
38
44
50

ONE

from A CHORUS LINE

TROMBONES

Music by MARVIN HAMLISCH
Lyric by EDWARD KLEBAN

17
20
23
26
29

POPULAR

from the Broadway Musical WICKED

TROMBONES

Music and Lyrics by
STEPHEN SCHWARTZ

21
25
29
33
37

SEASONS OF LOVE

from RENT

TROMBONES

Words and Music by
JONATHAN LARSON

13
16
19
23
27
1.
2.

SEVENTY SIX TROMBONES

from Meredith Willson's THE MUSIC MAN

TROMBONES

By MEREDITH WILLSON

29
1.
34
39
2.
44
49
55

SUMMERTIME

from PORGY AND BESS®

TROMBONES

Music and Lyrics by GEORGE GERSHWIN,
DuBOSE and DOROTHY HEYWARD
and IRA GERSHWIN

Slowly, with feeling (♫ = ♩♪ triplet)

17
21
24
28
32
rit.
rit.

SUNRISE, SUNSET

from the Musical FIDDLER ON THE ROOF

TROMBONES

Words by SHELDON HARNICK
Music by JERRY BOCK

29
34
39
45
51
56
rit.
rit.

TOMORROW

from the Musical Production ANNIE

TROMBONES

Lyric by MARTIN CHARNIN
Music by CHARLES STROUSE

13
16
19
22
rit.
rit.

WHERE IS LOVE?

from the Broadway Musical OLIVER!

TROMBONES

Words and Music by
LIONEL BART

16
19
22
25
29

YOU'VE GOT A FRIEND

featured in BEAUTIFUL: THE CAROLE KING MUSICAL

TROMBONES

Words and Music by
CAROLE KING

Moderately

20
24
28
31
34

HAL LEONARD PRESENTS

EASY INSTRUMENTAL DUETS

Start your duet playing experience with these fun songbooks! Over 20 easy duet arrangements for two instrumentalists are featured in each of these collections. Woodwind and brass editions can be played together as can the string editions. **Only $9.99 each!**

BROADWAY SONGS FOR TWO

22 showstoppers: Any Dream Will Do • Bring Him Home • Cabaret • Edelweiss • For Forever • Hello, Dolly! • I Believe • Memory • One • Popular • Seasons of Love • Seventy Six Trombones • Tomorrow • Where Is Love? • You've Got a Friend • and more.

00252493 FLUTE
00252494 CLARINET
00252495 ALTO SAX
00252496 TRUMPET
00252497 TROMBONE
00252500 VIOLIN
00252501 CELLO

CLASSICAL THEMES FOR TWO

24 favorite melodies from top classical composers: Air on the G String • Blue Danube Waltz • Canon in D • Eine Kleine Nachtmusik • Hallelujah Chorus • Jesu, Joy of Man's Desiring • Minuet in G Major • Ode to Joy • Pictures at an Exhibition • Sheep May Safely Graze • Trumpet Voluntary • William Tell Overture • and more.

00254439 FLUTE
00254440 CLARINET
00254441 ALTO SAX
00254442 TRUMPET
00254443 TROMBONE
00254444 VIOLIN
00254445 CELLO

CHRISTMAS HITS FOR TWO

22 terrific holiday duets: All I Want for Christmas Is You • Baby, It's Cold Outside • The Christmas Song (Chestnuts Roasting on an Open Fire) • Do You Want to Build a Snowman? • Feliz Navidad • Have Yourself a Merry Little Christmas • It's Beginning to Look like Christmas • Let It Snow! Let It Snow! Let It Snow! • Mary, Did You Know? • Rockin' Around the Christmas Tree • Silver Bells • White Christmas • and more.

00172461 FLUTE
00172462 CLARINET
00172463 ALTO SAX
00172464 TRUMPET
00172465 TROMBONE
00172466 VIOLIN
00172467 CELLO

HIT SONGS FOR TWO

22 mega hits: All About That Bass • All of Me • Brave • Can't Stop the Feeling • Grenade • Hey, Soul Sister • I Will Wait • Let Her Go • 100 Years • Royals • Shake It Off • Shape of You • Stay with Me • Viva La Vida • and more.

00252482 FLUTE
00252483 CLARINET
00252484 ALTO SAX
00252485 TRUMPET
00252486 TROMBONE
00252487 VIOLIN
00252488 CELLO

Prices, contents and availability subject to change without notice.
Sales restrictions to some countries apply.
All prices listed in U.S. funds.

ORDER TODAY FROM YOUR FAVORITE MUSIC RETAILER AT **HALLEONARD.COM**

HAL•LEONARD®

1217